THE HIGH PEAK OF THE VISION AND THE REALITY OF THE BODY OF CHRIST

Witness Lee

Living Stream Ministry
Anaheim, California • www.lsm.org

First Edition, November 1995.

ISBN 978-0-87083-935-1

Published by

Living Stream Ministry
2431 W. La Palma Ave., Anaheim, CA 92801 U.S.A.
P. O. Box 2121, Anaheim, CA 92814 U.S.A.

Printed in the United States of America

10   11   12   13   14   15   /   12   11   10   9   8   7   6   5

CONTENTS

PREFACE

This book is a translation of messages given in Chinese by Brother Witness Lee in his fellowship with the elders from Taipei on May 17-20, 1994 in Anaheim, California.

CHAPTER ONE

THE HIGH PEAK OF THE VISION

(1)

Prayer: O Lord, how we thank You for making it possible for us to have such a gathering. Lord, when we look back at the past up to the present time, we truly worship You, for everything depends on Your mercy and everything is done by Your mercy. As to ourselves, to this day we are still useless, still lacking, and still full of shortcomings before You. O Lord, what You have shown us is so much and so high, yet we have to admit before You that what we have practically entered into is very short. O Lord, we come, on the one hand, to worship You and thank You, and on the other hand, to confess to You our shortcomings and failures. Lord, grant us again Your visitation in these few days. We still look to You for Your mercy in fear and trembling. On our side, we are hopeless. O Lord, do cleanse us and anoint us. May You also bless us and guide us in our fellowship that we would not utter wasted words nor waste our time. We pray that You will support us.

O Lord, whenever we come into Your presence, as You taught us in Your prayer, we cannot forget that Your enemy is still here. We pray, Lord, that You would deliver us from his temptations. O Lord, may You truly enable us to overcome this evil one by the power of Your resurrection. O Lord, even more, we ask You to cover us with Your prevailing, precious blood and resist for us his attacks and disturbances. We further ask You to bind him for the sake of Your move on earth. O Lord, we pray that You would also remember our weakness. We are weak vessels; apart from You we can do nothing, we have nothing, and we are nothing. We can only worship You that You are everything. Amen.

Because you have all traveled by plane from so far away, I am very grateful within and also somewhat excited. Regretfully, I have not been to a meeting for three months. This is the first time in three months that I have gathered with you, brothers, for fellowship. I still feel that because of the need that is ahead of us, I cannot give you very much time. In these four nights, every night, besides the time for prayer, we will limit our time to one hour.

In the past three months I have had many, many things in me that I want to say to the churches in the Lord's recovery, and I do not believe I could finish speaking in three or four hundred messages. I sense that in these few nights the Lord wants me to hand over something to you. Tonight we will fellowship concerning the high peak of the vision that the Lord has shown us in these more than seventy years. Tomorrow night perhaps we will fellowship concerning the reality of the Body of Christ. At the end we may speak a word of warning and of being on the alert.

THE VISION AND REVELATION THAT THE LORD SHOWED US THROUGH BROTHER NEE

Thank the Lord that, according to what we know, as far as the history of the church and the existing state of the church are concerned, there has not been one age in which the Lord's revelation to His church has been as thorough and as high as what He has revealed to us in the past seventy-four years, beginning with Brother Nee. Through Brother Nee He first showed us the matter of salvation. In those days thousands of Western missionaries went to China. Many of them had quite a measure of spiritual worth and were quite learned. But not one Western missionary taught concerning the matter of salvation in a thorough, well-rounded way. This was the case until Brother Nee was raised up by the Lord. He not only preached the gospel, but he saw the salvation accomplished by the Lord according to His redemption, from the inside to the outside, from the beginning to the end, in a complete, well-rounded way, and he also handed over everything to us. You all know about this. If you want to know the details, you need to read Brother Nee's publications. For this reason we have compiled all his publications and printed them in three sets. Although you are all very busy, I still hope that you can read every page of those three sets.

Furthermore, through Brother Nee the Lord showed us the matter of the church. Concerning the church, the Lord showed us, on the negative side, that Christianity and Catholicism are altogether degraded and deformed. Never before had anyone spoken about the degradation of the Catholic Church and the Protestant churches in such a clear and thorough way as Brother Nee did. On the positive side, the Lord also led Brother Nee to see the local church, that is, the practical aspect of the church. He expended much effort in stressing this point. Eventually, the point of his emphasis became very clear. He enabled us to see clearly the ground of the church and the reality of the church.

Third, it was also through Brother Nee that God showed us the matter of Christ as our life. Christ is to be to us not only the Savior, the Redeemer, the Deliverer, the Grace-giver, and much more. These are not the center. The center is that Christ is to be our life. The Lord's redeeming, saving, and giving of grace are not the goal but the procedure to reach the goal. God's goal is Christ as our life. I say again, not only did the Western missionaries who went to China not stress this point; even in the entire history of Christianity only a handful paid attention to this point. This handful of people began mainly with Madame Guyon. Later, there were the mystics, and after them there were the inner-life people. Of course, Brother Nee stood on their shoulders, but Brother Nee saw something in a more thorough way and something higher, deeper, and richer than what they had seen.

After this God showed us the Body of Christ through Brother Nee. The Lord showed us that the local church is the procedure and not the goal. The goal of the local church is the building up of the Body of Christ. Here, regretfully, among us there were quite a number of brothers who were weighty, yet they saw only the importance of the local church and did not see the Body of Christ. Hence, they rose up to argue, saying that Brother Nee said very clearly that all local churches are autonomous, each having nothing to do with the others. Not one local church, whatever it may be, should interfere with another local church. This is their total disregard for the Body of Christ. Therefore, through Brother Nee the Lord showed us further that what God wants in the end is not the local church. Although at the end of the Bible there are seven lampstands, they all become one city, the New Jerusalem. However, those brothers who stressed the local aspect of the church insisted very much that what Revelation shows us in the beginning is individual churches. Moreover, they were influenced by the Brethren and considered that all the seven churches were different. However, their view is off the mark because they do not see that the seven golden lampstands are indistinguishable in nature, shape, and function. If we put the seven lampstands in front of us, unless we give each a number, it is impossible to tell which is which. Although Revelation 2 and 3 show us seven different churches, the biased brothers do not see that the differences among the churches are not on the positive side but on the negative side. The seven churches have their distinctive characteristics only in their negative conditions, such as their failures, degradation, mistakes, and shortages.

Not only so, Revelation does not have only three chapters. If we read on, first we see the overcomers. Although they are the overcomers in the local churches, in chapter twelve we see that they are one man-child, not seven man-children. In chapter fourteen we see that they are one group of 144,000 overcomers, not two groups, and much less seven groups. These 144,000 overcomers cannot possibly be out of one church. In the entire book of Revelation we see only one man-child, one group of overcomers. Furthermore, Peter was the apostle who set up the Jewish churches, and Paul was the apostle who set up the Gentile churches (Gal. 2:8). But at the end of Revelation the churches set up by the twelve apostles are one building, the holy city New Jerusalem, the Body of Christ.

The matter of salvation released by Brother Nee was received by everyone. People also received what he taught concerning the local church. As to the matter of Christ as our life, apparently people received what Brother Nee spoke, but in reality not many entered in. We must live with Christ day by day, receive Him as our life, take Him as our person in our daily life, and have a co-living with Him. But those who truly practice this, not to mention the outside Christians, even among the saints in the Lord's recovery, are as few as the morning stars. All of you are very sincere, and you have paid not a small price to travel from the other end of the world to be here. Since you have come with a sincere heart, I will speak to you a sincere word. May I ask you, among the approximately twenty of you, how many can say from your spirit, from your conscience, with full confidence, "I am a person who lives by Christ"? How many of you can say, "Regardless of whom I am dealing with, regardless of what I am doing, even in my clothing myself and my eating, even in speaking to my wife, in big things or small things, I always live with Christ, I do everything in the spirit and according to the spirit, and in my living I daily experience the Christ whom I have received and allow Him to be magnified in me"? In these three months while I was sick and was recuperating, I do not know how much I repented to the Lord regarding this matter. I cannot deny that I have seen this light most thoroughly. Since 1950 I have released numerous messages on this matter and have taught people about this. But when the Lord put me in quietness, I examined myself according to this light and found out that I have not really entered into it that much. What I have seen is very thorough, and what I have preached may also be considered quite complete, but it is really questionable how much of the reality of Christ as life I have in me. In this matter we all must enter in practically.

Although beginning from 1939 Brother Nee already saw the Body of Christ, his preaching concerning this matter was equivalent to "playing the piano to cows"; no one took it in. Therefore, the local churches everywhere just acted according to their own desire, even to the extent that Brother Nee was forced to stop his ministry. He stopped ministering for six years. In that period of six years, among us we had many who were capable of preaching, yet they did not see any vision or revelation. From 1942 to 1948, not one among us wrote a book that had any value or could be counted as anything. Our vision did not increase one bit; everything stopped there. Concerning the matter of the Body of Christ, many simply disagreed with it and completely ignored it. At the time of the turmoil in Shanghai in 1942, how many saw the Body of Christ? None. How could anyone who had seen the Body of Christ have stirred up that kind of turmoil? That would have been impossible.

After six years Brother Nee resumed his ministry. We have published a book recording solely the messages given by Brother Nee during the resumption of his ministry (see *Messages Given during the Resumption of Watchman Nee's Ministry,* published by Living Stream Ministry). The resumption of his ministry is very deeply related to me. In that book some of the messages were his and some of the messages were mine, and eventually it is difficult to distinguish between them. What was Brother Nee's emphasis in those messages? Brother Nee's messages, one after another, were on the Body of Christ. The problem among us lay in our not having seen the Body. In those messages Brother Nee was forced even to speak some very unpleasant words. He said that some churches were "native" churches; he also said that some churches were little kingdoms. This is what he said in the resumption of his ministry in June 1948. In March of that year I went especially to Foochow with several co-workers, including Brother K. H. Weigh, to fellowship with him. More than forty co-workers around us also desired to participate in the fellowship, but he refused all of them. Only two brothers, Brother Weigh and I, and two sisters, Peace Wang and Rachel Lee, were given permission to be with him. All the forty-odd co-workers waited in Foochow, and they asked me, saying, "Brother Lee, no matter what, please put in a word for us. We want to hear Brother Nee speak. We want to have a part." Brother Nee said, "No." It was as if I was asking for mercy before him. I said, "Look at all these brothers and sisters. Don't you care about them?" We were very sorrowful in our conversation. I asked for mercy again and again. Eventually he said, "Okay, Brother Witness, tell them to come." His house was quite large with a living room in two sections, an inner room and an outer room. At that time he gave his consent, not very willingly, saying, "Okay, ask them to come. Only the four of you will fellowship with me here in the inner room, and the rest of them must sit and listen in the outer room." Brother Nee began to fellowship with us. At that time I was the only one who spoke; the others would not speak. I said, "Brother Nee, look at the few dozens of churches here in Fukien Province. They are in confusion and are scattered. What shall we do?" So he began to speak, and that message touched every one of us. Then Sister Wang, who was in the outer room, said, "Why don't we practice what you have told us?" After some consideration Brother Nee said, "If you want to practice it, every one of you must hand over himself. You must hand over everything: hand over yourself, hand over your family, hand over your riches, hand over your church, hand over everything." It was from that time that the practice of handing over began. This was three months before he resumed his ministry and spoke concerning the "native" churches and little kingdoms. Not too long after these things, he was put into prison. He was kept in prison for twenty years, from 1952 to 1972, and eventually he became a martyr.

After the resumption of his ministry, he still came to take the lead in the Lord's recovery. Then at the end of 1948 the political situation changed. So he called an urgent meeting in Shanghai with a dozen or so leading co-workers. He said, "Today I asked you to come here. You all know the world situation is changing. When facing the world situation, how should we handle it?" Before anyone said anything, he said, "First, I would like to make a statement. We will send Brother Witness abroad." Afterward, at the conclusion of the meeting, Brother Nee said, "We all will remain here to seek the Lord's leading. May the Lord lead us one by one." I did not say anything. He charged me to quickly finish building the big meeting hall in Shanghai. At that time we had bought a piece of land for the building of the meeting hall; that was in November. After another three months Brother Nee called another meeting and gave the same opening word, saying, "I will say this first: We will ask Brother Witness to go abroad."

This time he said that we did not need to seek guidance but should all stay to be sacrificed for the Lord. He said that of course we should look to the Lord to preserve us. But he was afraid that one day when we would go on and risk our lives, we would all be "captured in one net." Both of the co-workers' meetings were very short and both took place at dusk. While the sisters were preparing dinner for us, I took the opportunity to take a little walk with Brother Nee outside the house. I said to him sorrowfully, "Brother Nee, why is it that you want only me to go abroad, yet you all are staying here to risk your lives for the Lord? Is it because I am not worthy?" He turned around and looked at me, saying, "Brother Witness, you have to know that we will risk our lives for the Lord, but I am afraid that one day Satan will capture us in one net. If you go out, and if one day this thing really happens, we will still have something remaining." I can never forget that word.

After two months he asked me to hand over everything of the church in Shanghai to the elders and he told me to leave the country. So I left. I first went to Taiwan. Then he was imprisoned for twenty years. There was a person who was his prison mate and much younger than he and who was led to salvation in the prison through Brother Nee. He could be considered a spiritual son of Brother Nee, and he also treated Brother Nee as his father. This brother, whose family name is Wu, got out of the prison first. Not too long before his death, Brother Nee had told this brother, "After you go out, you should try to find a brother by the name of Witness Lee. Tell him that I have not abandoned my faith. When you see him, you see me. What he speaks to you, that is my speaking to you." This is what the niece of Brother Nee and her husband, Dr. Kung, heard when they met this Brother Wu in Shanghai. I can never forget Brother Nee's word to me that "if you go out, we will still have something remaining." Therefore, today if you go to my bedroom, you will notice that there is no other picture in my bedroom except the picture of Brother Nee. Furthermore, there is also a writing by Brother Nee on "Let me love and not be appreciated" hanging on one side of my bedroom. I miss him and I will always miss him.

THE TURNING OF THE LORD'S REVELATION AND VISION
AND THE ARRIVING AT THE HIGH PEAK

In Brother Nee the Lord's revelation and vision reached the Body of Christ. It is a wonderful coincidence that at about the time he went into prison in 1952, the Lord began to use me in Taiwan. From 1950 to this day, it has been forty-four years. Do not blame me for speaking a proud word; I am not proud. You know on what point I began in these forty-four years. I began with Christ and the church. Many of the messages concerning these two points have been published in book form. Among these a good number of the messages are on the Body of Christ. Then a little over ten years ago, probably from 1980, the Lord showed me that in order to have the Body of Christ, the dispensing of Christ is indispensable. So I began to speak concerning the dispensing of Christ. If Christ does not dispense Himself into us, how can we become His Body? From that point I went higher and saw the economy of God. Hence, beginning from 1984 I released many messages on the economy of God. Then in the spring of this year (actually I saw it last year) I continued to go higher. I saw that it is only by God's becoming man to make man God that the Body of Christ can be produced. This point is the high peak of the vision given to us by God.

Actually, early in the fourth century Athanasius, who was present at the Nicene Council, said that "He was made man that we might be made God." At that time he was an unnoticed young theologian. This word of his became a maxim in church history. However, later, gradually people in Christianity not only would not teach this but did not dare to teach this.

God is God, and He Himself has begotten us as His children. Whatever anything is born of, that is what it is. We cannot say that when sheep beget sheep, the old sheep are sheep but the little sheep are not sheep. Since God has begotten us, we are the children of God. Furthermore, 1 John 3 says that God will work on us to such an extent that we will be like Him completely (v. 2). From the day God created man, this has been the purpose of God. Hence, what He created was man, yet He created man with the image of God. Adam was created with God's image and likeness. Then God set man before the tree of life, meaning that He wanted man, who had God's image, to receive God as his life. As a result, if a man who has received God as his life is not God, then what is he? But the Lord also shows us clearly that we are God in life and nature. A father begets a son, and this son surely is the same as the father in life and nature. Suppose the father is an emperor. We cannot say that all his children are emperors. The children have only their father's life and nature but not his status; this is clear. God did this that He might produce a Body for Christ, that is, that He might produce an organism for the Triune God, the ultimate manifestation of which is the New Jerusalem.

In the Chinese-speaking conference in February of this year, the brothers wanted me to speak, and my burden was to speak about this matter. For twenty-seven years I had not written a new hymn. Several days before the Chinese-speaking conference I wrote a new hymn with four stanzas:

1   What miracle! What mystery!
    That God and man should blended be!
    God became man to make man God,
    Untraceable economy!
    From His good pleasure, heart's desire,
    His highest goal attained will be.

2   Flesh He became, the first God-man,
    His pleasure that I God may be:
    In life and nature I'm God's kind,
    Though Godhead's His exclusively.
    His attributes my virtues are;
    His glorious image shines through me.

3   No longer I alone that live,
    But God together lives with me.
    Built with the saints in the Triune God,
    His universal house we'll be,
    And His organic Body we
    For His expression corp'rately.

4 Jerusalem, the ultimate,
    Of visions the totality;
    The Triune God, tripartite man—
    A loving pair eternally—
    As man yet God they coinhere,
    A mutual dwelling place to be;
    God's glory in humanity
    Shines forth in splendor radiantly!

After singing this hymn, you can realize that it is a special hymn. In the two-thousand-year history of Christianity there is not one hymn that is of this category. This is the unique hymn in this category of hymns. This hymn speaks very clearly concerning the high peak of God's vision.

Today in the Lord's recovery, it is not that we will not preach the gospel anymore; but preaching the gospel is for begetting. And it is not that we will not nourish the saints anymore or that we will not perfect the saints anymore. All the begetting, nourishing, and perfecting are for the building. However, what are we building? Are we just building the local churches? No. We are building the local churches for the building up of the Body of Christ, which will consummate in the New Jerusalem. Then, does this mean that we just forget about the local churches? No. The local churches are the procedure for God to accomplish the building of the Body of Christ. God still has to greatly use the local churches. Thank the Lord, through this kind of fellowship I hope that we all know where we are today and also where we should be and what we should do.

THE HIGH PEAK OF THE VISION

(2)

Prayer: O Lord, only You know our need. We need to see You; we need to see Your economy, Your goal, and Your heart's desire. O Lord, we worship You. Everything on our side depends on Your mercy. You will have mercy on whomever You will have mercy. O Lord! We pray that You will continue to have mercy on us and go on further to have mercy on us. O Lord, Your church has been on the earth for more than nineteen hundred years, yet her condition is still as it is today. O Lord, we pray that You will deliver us from this religious age that we may truly enter into the state which You are after in Your economy. O Lord, cleanse us and anoint us again tonight. We pray also that You will cover us with Your precious blood and remove for us all disturbance and confusion. Give us the words and purify our words. Lord, we worship You in that You have destroyed Your enemy. Amen.

"GOD BECAME MAN THAT MAN MAY BECOME GOD" BEING THE ESSENCE OF THE ENTIRE BIBLE

I sense that I still need to fellowship with you brothers concerning the matter of the vision. Tonight we want to see the matter of "God became man that man may become God" in the economy of God. The words "God becoming man and man becoming God" sound very simple, but to be able to see how God could become man requires us to spend much time to study. He came to become man that man may become Him, but how can man become God? We also need to look into this point carefully. Strictly speaking, these words are the essence of the entire Bible. The entire Bible is an explanation of the eternal economy of God. Up to the present time it has been thirty-five hundred years since the Jews began to read the Old Testament; Christians have been reading the Old and New Testaments for nearly two thousand years. Millions of people have read the Bible. However, unfortunately, not many have truly seen the proper significance and real meaning in the Bible. This does not mean that throughout the generations no one has seen the visions in the Bible; but what people saw is fragmented. One saw a little concerning one aspect, and another saw a little concerning another aspect. Hence, among all the departments of the human race in the whole world, Christianity has the greatest number of books. That no other department in the world has more books than Christianity is proof that many people have seen something from the Bible.

BROTHER NEE'S MINISTRY AND
HIS ARRANGEMENT CONCERNING THE WORK

When the Lord raised us up in China, He showed us the entire vision in the Bible in a brief and concise way through Brother Nee, the main points of which I fellowshipped with you in the previous chapter: the salvation of God, the church, Christ as life, and the Body of Christ. These are the things that Brother Nee saw clearly and spoke to us in the thirty years of his ministry. I say again that, unfortunately, of these four great points that he showed us, the average brother and sister understood only the first three points and disagreed with the last point, that is, the Body of Christ. At any rate, from 1922 to 1952, when he was put into prison, Brother Nee carried out his ministry for exactly thirty years. Then, in the twenty years after 1952 he was not able to write any book or do any work.

In 1950, before Brother Nee was put into prison, the Lord led him to make an arrangement among the co-workers, an arrangement that was unequaled before or after. He rarely made this kind of arrangement because at that time the political situation kept changing and we did not know how to prepare ourselves for the change. In the two urgent co-workers' meetings he repeatedly said, "We ask Brother Witness to go abroad." Afterward, when the Communists gained the upper hand, I was in Shanghai hurrying to finish the building of the big meeting hall, and the only job left to be done was to install the flooring composed of small marble chips set in cement. At the end of April 1949, Brother Nee sent me a wire telling me to turn over everything of the church in Shanghai to the elders and leave immediately. Thus, I was sent out.

THE TRANSFER OF THE MINISTRY IN THE LORD'S RECOVERY AND THE BEGINNING OF THE WORK IN TAIWAN

After I arrived in Taiwan, outside the house I heard the noise of wooden shoes on the gravel road, and inside the house I saw a room with Japanese tatami. At that time there were at most fifty people meeting in Taipei, and there was not much for me to do. I lay in bed in my home looking at the ceiling, saying, "What did I come to Taiwan for?" That was in April. Later I took a trip to the central and southern parts of Taiwan. The Lord gave me a sense that something could be done in Taiwan and that it was a very good place in which it was easy to set up local churches, because in one day I could go to three or four places and the transportation was very convenient. Therefore, on August 1, 1949, I officially began the work in Taiwan.

The next year Brother Nee went to Hong Kong. In the beginning of the year a revival was brought in, so he asked me to go to Hong Kong to help him lead the whole church in Hong Kong in three aspects of service: the service of the co-workers, the service of the elders, and the service of the deacons. For a period of one and a half months the two of us were there, and nearly every day we met with each group. From the end of 1949, for two years the church in Shanghai enjoyed complete freedom. Brother Nee had never before had such a great opportunity to release what he had received of the Lord, because at that time all the Western missionaries had left. At that time ninety percent of Chinese Christianity was in the hands of the Western missionaries, so after they left, the different denominations in Shanghai were like flocks without shepherds, and anyone who had a little desire to pursue the Lord turned to us. Brother Nee considered that a golden opportunity. In 1962 or 1963 Brother Nee's brother-in-law Samuel Chang told me, "Brother Lee, in 1950, before Brother Nee left for Hong Kong to hold a conference there, the co-workers in Shanghai talked about transferring you out of Taiwan, since there was not much to be done in Taiwan. They wanted you to return to Shanghai, where there was too much work to be done. As far as Christianity was concerned, the entire Shanghai was in our hands."

Brother Nee was very wise; he seldom did things or said things in a rush or in a headstrong way but always tried to see how God would lead and arrange in the environment. Therefore, when I arrived in Hong Kong, he did not mention this thing to me. As we sat down to talk, spontaneously I told him about the situation of the work in Taiwan in that half year or more. I told him that up to the end of the preceding year the number in the church in Taipei had increased thirty times. In my speaking I also showed that I was very burdened, saying that from there we could go to work in Southeast Asia, and then go on to East Asia, and gradually we could go on to the West. After hearing me speak concerning the situation in Taiwan, he not only did not bring up the matter decided by the co-workers in mainland China about transferring me back to the mainland, but he also encouraged me to do a good job. We talked about going back to mainland China. I said, "This is too great a matter; I don't dare to say that either going back or not going back is the Lord's will." He said, "What shall we do with the few hundred churches?" After a few days, without saying good-bye to anyone, he went back to mainland China. More than ten days later, after he left Hong Kong I also returned to Taiwan.

When I went to Taiwan, I had a family of ten with two domestic helpers. A total of twelve went to Taiwan. When I got off the plane, I had three hundred U.S. dollars with me. Brother Nee fully realized the situation among us, and he knew that when I arrived in Taiwan it would be difficult for me to receive support. At that time there were only a handful of saints in Taiwan, and most of them went there to take refuge, so they did not have much to spare to support others. Brother Nee truly loved the co-workers; he said, "Brother Witness, here I have a bottle of medicine as a sample, and I also have the formula. Take these two things back to Taiwan. Gather some brothers who are engaging in business and ask them to make a small investment and do a little advertising. That would be enough." So I went back to Taiwan and fellowshipped with the brothers, but everyone felt that it was not the proper time, so we did not do it.

At the end of 1950 I went to Manila. I worked there for five and a half months, and just before I left, a brother went to the elders and asked them to make an appointment for him to see me. This brother was a businessman and was quite wealthy but had donated little prior to that time. He came to see me and said, "Brother Lee, now you are going back to Taiwan. Please tell me the total amount of the annual expenses of your work in Taiwan, including the building of meeting halls and the support for the co-workers. I have the burden before the Lord to bear the whole responsibility." This was truly something of the Lord's doing. Then I said, "Brother Wang, you know the practice among us is that we do not tell people of our needs." He said, "This is not you telling me, but it is I receiving the Lord's commission. Therefore, if you don't tell me, how can I know the amount?" So I told him. Thus, he supplied the work every year for eleven years, from 1950 to 1961; every year there was a sum of money as a supply. Thank the Lord, this was all His doing.

I went back from Manila to Taiwan. At that time I was the only full-time brother in Taiwan, and there was a Sister Hou, who was also serving full-time. On the whole island of Taiwan we were the only two full-time serving ones. Even Brothers Chang Wu-chen and Sun Feng-lu were not yet full-time. Everyone knew that unless he went to get a job, there would be no support, so everyone got a job. After I had this experience in Southeast Asia, I fellowshipped with the brothers. Then I began to hold trainings. In 1952 over eighty full-time serving ones were produced. I told the church clearly that it did not mean that the churches had no responsibility or that the brothers and sisters did not need to give in love. But my own experience told me that there was the possibility that the serving ones would have no food on their tables. From the Bible we see that this was also the experience of Paul. Therefore, I said that, because of my experience, the support which I received in the work of my ministry would be used to pay the expenses of providing adequate food for the co-workers and their families. This means that even if the brothers and sisters would not give anything, the co-workers still would have food on their tables. This support continued through 1961. From 1961 the churches began to share according to their ability in order to reduce the burden on the side of my work. Because many churches were set up and the number of saints increased, they reduced the amount of my support of the co-workers to about sixty percent. Thus, gradually, in 1964 I unloaded this burden. All this was recorded in the accounts of the Gospel Book Room in those years. The number of co-workers with their families reached a peak of 170. Every year the ministry supplied them for their daily needs. This was truly the Lord's doing.

In 1950 I had my last contact with Brother Nee. At the time I was not clear, but now when I look back, I see that it was the Lord's doing; that is, the Lord was making preparations to transfer to me the ministry of the word in the Lord's recovery. When I was in mainland China, I did not publish books on my own. Rather, I helped Brother Nee manage the Gospel Book Room. I wrote only a few articles, which Brother Nee liked and published as a book, entitled *Gleanings from Christ's Genealogy*. There were also a few other books concerning the kingdom of the heavens. In 1950, when the two of us were in Hong Kong, we spent much time talking together. Because I realized that later it might not be possible for me to contact Brother Nee, I brought up to him the need to publish in Taiwan. He said, "Brother Witness, you know that among us only I personally own the Gospel Book Room. It belongs neither to the church nor to the co-workers; it belongs to me personally." Then he made arrangements, saying, "Now the three political regions—the mainland, Hong Kong, and Taiwan—all differ from one another. So we will have the Gospel Book Room divided into three: one in Shanghai, one in Taiwan, and one in Hong Kong. They are not three Book Rooms; rather, they are one. Due to the political situation, the three places will be on their own financially." He was responsible for the one in Shanghai; he entrusted to me the responsibility for the one in Taiwan; and he asked Brother K. H. Weigh to take charge of the one in Hong Kong. He further charged me, saying, "Brother Weigh also needs your help in bearing the responsibility for the articles." Therefore, in the initial period, the Taiwan Gospel Book Room published books mainly in coordination with the Book Room in Hong Kong. The two published books together, not separately. The cost of the books published both in Hong Kong and Taiwan were calculated together. It was due to such an arrangement made by Brother Nee that we have today's situation.

Thank the Lord, as soon as we began the work in Taipei, an overseas Chinese brother contributed ten thousand U.S. dollars, and that became the beginning of the Gospel Book Room. Concerning the Book Room, I have explained clearly to the co-workers that this Book Room does not belong to the church nor to the co-workers nor to the work. Just as it was in the past with Brother Nee, this is my book room to serve the publication of my ministry. Therefore, I began to publish books in Taiwan. I knew that there could no longer be the ministry that was with Brother Nee and we could no longer have it. So I began to carry out the literature work in Taiwan. That fellowship in Hong Kong truly was the Lord's sovereign arrangement in that Brother Nee gave me instructions concerning the work. After another two years he was put into prison. In 1952 in Taiwan over eighty full-time serving ones were added at the same time. I can testify to you that none of these things was of my work, but everything was the Lord's sovereign arrangement. From 1932, when I began to speak for the Lord, to the year 1952 was a total of twenty years. I began to speak ten years later than Brother Nee. Brother Nee began to speak for the Lord in 1922. From that time to the summer of 1952, when he was imprisoned, he spoke for a total of thirty years. From 1952 on, the Lord transferred the ministry of the word to me.

THE ADVANCING AND ASCENDING OF THE MINISTRY
OF THE WORD IN THE LORD'S RECOVERY

From the monthly publication *The Ministry of the Word* you can see that we were still shallow. From 1951 to 1961, ten years went by. Then I had a burden. I sensed that our hymnal was lacking and could not match the vision that we saw, so I compiled a supplemental hymnal containing eighty-five new hymns which I wrote within two months' time. In our hymnal, hymns such as #499, the first line of which reads, "Oh, what a life! Oh, what a peace! / The Christ who's all within me lives," and #501, "O glorious Christ, Savior mine, / Thou art truly radiance divine," were written at that time. I am surprised that over thirty years ago I was able to write hymns such as #499 and #501. I am even more surprised that not too long afterward I was able to write #203, "In the bosom of the Father, / Ere the ages had begun, / Thou wast in the Father's glory, / God's unique begotten Son. / When to us the Father gave Thee, / Thou in person wast the same, / All the fulness of the Father / In the Spirit to proclaim." Stanza three says that the Lord was the only grain, and then stanza four says we are His reproduction, His Body and His bride. It is surprising that over thirty years ago I could write such a hymn. What I saw then of the Lord was based on what Brother Nee had seen. What I saw then was just that much. In those eighty-five hymns my emphases were Christ, the Body of Christ, the Spirit, and life. Since then, after another period of time, the Lord's table meeting among us turned from the old hymns to the new hymns. Formerly, in the old hymns we remembered mainly the Lord's love, the Lord's death, the Lord's redemption, etc. But now in nearly every Lord's table meeting what we select are these new hymns. Our praise to the Lord is thus uplifted and enriched.

The year 1952 was a turning point for me in the ministry of the word, and 1962 was another turning point. After that I came to the United States. At that time—may the Lord cover me with His precious blood—I became quite mature in the ministry of the word. Two months ago the church here was getting into the life-study of Hebrews as *The Holy Word for Morning Revival*. The life-study of Hebrews was given by

me in 1975, exactly nineteen years ago. I expounded the book
of Hebrews in a high and profound way and not one portion
needs to be revised. This is to show you that in 1961 when
I came to the United States I was already quite mature in
the ministry of the word. For almost fifteen to twenty years
all that I ministered was Christ, the Spirit, life, and the
church. At that time I also saw the building of the Body of
Christ. One of the new hymns I wrote, #840, is on the building
of the Body of Christ. This hymn says, "Freed from self and
Adam's nature, / Lord, I would be built by Thee." Today when
I sing this hymn, I still sense that it is so fresh and so full of
light.

After nearly twenty years, the Lord began to lead me into
seeing the dispensing of the Triune God and the eternal
economy of God. In the recent ten years and more, what
the Lord has been continually showing me is this matter.
Then it was during this year (1994), in the new year's Chinese-
speaking conference, that I saw the peak. Based on what I
saw, I wrote a new hymn representing the high peak of the
vision which the Lord has shown us: "What miracle! What
mystery! / That God and man should blended be! / God became
man to make man God, / Untraceable economy! / From His
good pleasure, heart's desire, / His highest goal attained will
be." Formerly among us we did not even have such words, but
now these words have been written into a hymn.

GOD BECOMING MAN AND MAN BECOMING GOD

"God becoming man and man becoming God" is the economy of God; it is beyond the comprehension of angels and
men. This is the point that I want to cover tonight. The
Scriptures tell us clearly that God became a man to be our
Savior and then He redeemed and regenerated us. Orthodox
Christians and fundamental teachers all have seen these
truths. However, they do not see that there is a line concerning the economy of God recorded in the Scriptures showing us
how God became man to make man God. The Bible shows
us how man can become God to have a God-man living and
thus become an organism of God, which is the Body of Christ.
This is something that they do not see.

GOD BECOMING MAN—
GOING THROUGH THE CREATION OF MAN
AND HIS COMING PERSONALLY TO BECOME MAN

Tonight I would like to spend some time to speak on how God became man. For God to become man, first He had to create man. God created man according to His image and likeness; this is the shell. Although what God created was man, this man whom He created had the image of God. This is the first step. In the next step, God personally came to be a man. How did He come to be a man? He did this by entering into humanity. Physically, this means that He entered into a human virgin to be conceived in her. Matthew 1 says that God was begotten in Mary. According to the law in God's creation, He was conceived in Mary's womb and remained there for nine months. Then after He stayed in humanity for nine months, He was born out of humanity with divinity. The man who was born was One who is God yet man and who is also man yet God. Christianity has Christmas, Christianity has the manger, and Christianity has the angels announcing the good news. But concerning what I have just presented to you in a simple way, Christianity does not have a clear seeing. As such a God-man He passed through human living on the earth and lived a human life. How did He live such a life? He did it by depending on His divine life within and by rejecting His human life without and thus living the life of a God-man. The inner reality of such a God-man living was the divine attributes, and the outward living that was lived out of such a God-man living was the human virtues. By thus living the life of a God-man He became a typical example.

However, it is not enough for God to have just one man as a typical example, a model. God needs a mass manifestation. Therefore, eventually, He went to the cross. When He went to the cross, He brought with Him the man whom He had become; that is, He put on this man and thus crucified this man. This death of His was an all-inclusive death. This death of His was the death of a fallen man, a sinful man. When He became a man, He did not become a God-created man or a holy man; rather, He became a God-created yet fallen man. His flesh was the flesh of sin, except there was no poison of

sin, no substance of sin, within it. It was merely in the likeness of the flesh of sin. Therefore, Romans 8:3 says that He
came in the likeness of the flesh of sin. He was such a man.
Hence, what He brought to the cross to be crucified there
was also such a man. Through crucifixion He terminated the
man of the old creation on the cross. The man of the old
creation involves all created things. Therefore, His death also
terminated everything of the old creation on the cross. The
man of the old creation also had sin, so His death on the cross
also took away sin. Furthermore, Satan was hidden in the
flesh of this sinful man. Therefore, Christ's death on the
cross not only crucified the flesh but also destroyed Satan
(Heb. 2:14). However, His crucifixion was not the end; rather,
He was resurrected from death. How was He resurrected? He
was resurrected through the power of His divine life with the
humanity that He had put on, the part created by God. In His
resurrection He brought humanity into divinity.

Through His incarnation God brought divinity into humanity, and through His resurrection He brought humanity
into divinity. Incarnation is the crucial step He took to bring
divinity into humanity. Then, later, in His resurrection He
brought the humanity which He had put on into divinity.
Thus, the God-created human nature was uplifted. Originally,
God was not in the human nature which He created. But now
He was resurrected, and all the God-chosen people were
resurrected in Him. His resurrection was to bring the
God-created humanity into divinity to be resurrected with
Him. This is why we say that the human nature was uplifted.
Andrew Murray said the same thing, except that the wording
he used is different from ours and not as thorough as ours. In
this resurrection He brought the humanity which He had put
on into divinity and thus became God's firstborn Son. His
becoming the Firstborn was His birth in His resurrection.
This is why, concerning Christ's resurrection, Acts 13:33 says,
"You are My Son; today I have begotten You." He was already
the Son of God, except that He did not have the human
nature in Him. When He became the firstborn Son, He not
only had divinity as His life, but He also had the uplifted
humanity added to His divinity. It is in the mingling of the

two natures that He became God's firstborn Son. Thus, He was begotten to be God's firstborn Son, and at the same time He regenerated all the God-chosen people (1 Pet. 1:3). To use our ordinary language, we may say that we and the Lord as God's firstborn Son were born in the same delivery. We all were born together in Christ's resurrection. This birth of His was the first step as a foundation for man to become God. Now in His resurrection, we as God's chosen ones have been brought into divinity. Thus, through regeneration we have received another life.

Not only so, He as the last Adam, who in His resurrection brought humanity into divinity, became the life-giving Spirit (1 Cor. 15:45). Who is this life-giving Spirit? He is the consummation of the processed Triune God. This is just like brewing a cup of tea. When you brew a cup of tea, first you need to have some water, then you put the tea in, and finally you add some lemon and maybe some sugar. At this point, the tea has been consummated. Christ as God's only begotten Son may be likened to plain water. At a certain time human nature was added to Him. Then, when He was put to death on the cross, the element of the effectiveness of His death was also added. Furthermore, He entered into resurrection, so the element of resurrection with its power was also added. Now, as God's only begotten Son He has become God's firstborn Son, and the many sons of God were born together with Him.

Besides the element of His divinity, Christ had the elements of His humanity, His experience of human living, and His death and resurrection added into Him. Thus, He became a life-giving Spirit. This Spirit is the consummation of the Triune God. This Spirit is also the pneumatic Christ, who is the embodiment of the Triune God. Hence, this Spirit is the very Christ, the very Triune God. Eventually, our God has become such a One. From the day of His resurrection to eternity He will be like this eternally. When we believe in the Lord, the One whom we receive is such a One, not a shallow Christ as people commonly preach. The Christ whom we know is so profound and so high. This One is our Redeemer and our Savior. He is not only Jesus Christ but also the One who became the life-giving Spirit, the consummation of God. It is this One who went through all these processes to accomplish the step for Him to become man that He might make man God.

MAN BECOMING GOD —
GOING THROUGH REGENERATION, SANCTIFICATION, RENEWING, TRANSFORMATION, CONFORMATION, AND GLORIFICATION

Then how does God make man God? After God regenerates us with Himself as life, He continues to carry out the work of sanctification, renewing, and transformation in us by His Spirit of life. God became man through incarnation; man becomes God through transformation. When the Lord Jesus lived as a man on this earth, once He went up on the mountain and was transfigured. That transfiguration was a sudden occurrence. Our transformation into God, however, is not something that happens unexpectedly. Rather, it is a lifetime transformation until we are conformed to His image. Eventually, we will enter with Him into glory; that is, we will be redeemed in our body. That will be the final step of the redemption of our whole being that brings us into glory. Therefore, it is through regeneration, sanctification, renewing, transformation, conformation, and glorification that we may become God. When we reach this point, 1 John 3:2 says that when "He is manifested, we will be like Him because we will see Him even as He is."

The issue of this process is an organism. This organism is God joining and mingling Himself with man to make God man and also to make man God. Among the Divine Trinity, as far as the Father is concerned, this organism is the house of the Father, the house of God; as far as the Son is concerned, it is the Body of Christ. The house is for God to have a dwelling place, whereas the Body is for God to have an expression. The ultimate issue is the New Jerusalem. This shows us how God became man and how afterward He makes man God that man may live a God-man life. The God-man life that we live today is the model life that Jesus Christ lived on earth by going through death and resurrection. In the Gospel of John the human life of Jesus Christ on earth was a life before death and resurrection. In the Epistles the Christian life, the life of a God-man, that we live is a life after death and resurrection. In resurrection we are being transformed daily.

Even among us, very few have entered deeply into these mysteries of the Divine Trinity as life. May the Lord have mercy on us. I hope that through this word of fellowship we all may be able to see this vision and pursue to enter into the reality of this vision.

CHAPTER THREE

THE REALITY OF THE BODY OF CHRIST

(1)

Prayer: O Lord, we pray that You will open our eyes
that we may really know You, how You as merely God were
incarnated, lived a human life, were crucified, and entered
into resurrection to become the consummated God with
divinity, humanity, the experiences of human living, and the
effectiveness of death and resurrection. Lord, You are such a
One. You have become the Spirit, and today You live in us to
carry out a particular work in us to make us God. O Lord, we
pray that You will cause us to see. We want this kind of
seeing. O Lord, only Your light can kill us, and only Your light
can eliminate all our doings. Lord, we need Your mercy; do
really shine within us.

May You speak to us today, even with an abundance
of light, that we may not merely apprehend or understand.
What we need is to see. We receive You as light. Forgive us
again for our shortcomings and mistakes and for our not
being absolute and our not being faithful. We really need
Your forgiveness. We have also done numerous things without
You, for all of which we need Your forgiveness and the cleans-
ing of Your precious blood. We cannot depend on any merit or
any integrity and perfection of our own. O Lord, we can be
accepted by You and live in Your fellowship only by Your precious blood. It is also by Your precious blood that we can
overcome our accusing enemy. O Lord, because Your enemy is
always on our heels, we can only declare that we overcome
him by the blood of the Lamb. Lord, grant us a good fellowship. Amen.

Brothers, I really have the burden to fellowship with you
concerning one thing, that is, how God became man and also

how He makes man God. The issue of this matter of God becoming man and man becoming God is an organism. This organism is the union and mingling of God with man, and this organism is also the Body of Christ. This is what we want to fellowship tonight. After this, we will go on to see the reality of the Body of Christ.

GOD BECAME MAN TO MAKE MAN GOD

First, we will speak concerning God becoming man to make man God. According to what is clearly recorded in the Scriptures, today Christians in general know that, first, God was incarnated; second, He came to live a human life; third, He was crucified; and fourth, He entered into resurrection. These four points are common things in Christianity; everyone knows them. Everyone knows that this incarnated One is Jesus, with the four Gospels as His biographical sketches. This Jesus lived a human life for thirty-three and a half years; then He was put to death on the cross, and after three days He was resurrected. These four points are so common that they are known even by some non-Christians. We need to see, however, that what people generally know about these four points is altogether superficial and is according to the letter. When they read and reread the New Testament, all people see is something in letter, something literal. They have seen that the New Testament, especially the four Gospels, is concerned with Christ's birth, Christ's life and walk on the earth, Christ's death, and Christ's resurrection. Therefore, they invent Christmas and the announcing of the good news to declare that Christ was born in a manger in Bethlehem to be the Savior of the world. They know only this much; nearly no one knows the real significance of the incarnation of God.

Today, some seminary professors and some renowned evangelists teach people concerning the stories of Jesus: how He opened the eyes of the blind and made the lame walk, how He loved people and received the little ones, and how He calmed the wind and the sea and raised the dead. They talk a lot about these things, but they do not really see the real meaning of Christ's human living. Preachers preach mainly that Christ died for us to make propitiation for our sins, that

He loves us and even gave Himself up for us. Besides this they do not have much to say.

The mystics, the inner life people, began in the seventeenth century. At that time some of them, including Madame Guyon, still remained in the Roman Catholic Church. As a mystic, Madame Guyon spoke in a very mysterious way that was too difficult for people to comprehend. Later, in the following century, a brother by the name of William Law was raised up in England. He was originally a mystic, and it was he who improved the teachings of mysticism and made them simple and easy to understand. Andrew Murray followed him. By reading the books of William Law, which simplified the mystical teachings, Andrew Murray received help, so he went on further to preach those truths. His preaching was very good, and he produced a masterpiece entitled *The Spirit of Christ*. Some in Christianity had already translated that book into Chinese, but the translation was not very clear. So when I was in Taipei I urged several young people to re-translate it and I completely revised the translation. To this day it is still not easy to read that book.

After Andrew Murray two lines emerged. On the one hand there was Mrs. Penn-Lewis. She focused on the death of Christ, stressing its negative aspect. She showed us how Christ's death dealt with our old man, crossed out our flesh, and destroyed Satan. Her speaking was excellent. We may say that she can be considered the first since the dawn of history who spoke concerning the death of Christ in such a profound yet practical way. On the other hand, there was Brother Austin-Sparks, who undoubtedly saw the principle of resurrection. Concerning the resurrection of Christ, his speaking was also excellent, yet it was rather mysterious and not easily comprehended. Over sixty years ago I read a book written by him entitled *The Release of the Lord*. What I read was a pamphlet in English, since it was not translated into Chinese yet. That book tells us that the death of Christ not only solved our problems on the negative side but also released the divine life within Him on the positive side. The divine life that He released is He Himself. Hence, that book stresses that Christ was the grain of wheat that died in order to release the life within it and thus produce many grains. I was helped very much.

That book actually is on the resurrection of Christ. The death of Christ is a termination. It put an end to man so that everything related to man—the old creation, sin, Satan, and the world—was also ended with the ending of man. Brother Austin-Sparks showed us that the termination of everything of the old creation is only the first half of the death of Christ, which is the negative aspect. The latter half of the death of Christ is positive, which was to release Himself (who is God), His divinity, and His divine life. One time in the Gospels the Lord Jesus said that He was constrained and He longed to die in order to be released (Luke 12:50). Christ died, and through His death the shell of His flesh, which He put upon Himself when He became man, was broken. This is just like the grain of wheat that was sown into the earth and died, thereby completely destroying the shell of the wheat. Out from the wheat, life was released and sprouts were brought forth; thus, many grains were produced. We are those grains. Later, following what Brother Austin-Sparks said, I went on further to say that these grains are ground into powder to form one loaf, which is the Body of Christ.

THE HUMAN VIRTUES OF JESUS
EXPRESSING THE DIVINE ATTRIBUTES

We need to see that the death of Christ has not only a negative aspect but also a positive aspect. The positive aspect was to release Him as God. That the Lord Jesus was God was concealed for thirty-three and a half years in His flesh, in His human form. In His life on earth of thirty-three and a half years, a great part of His living was the manifestation of His inner divine attributes. What was manifested became His human virtues. Today, the common readers of the Scriptures see only that Jesus was very good and full of virtues. But very few people see what the essence of the virtues of the Lord Jesus is. The essence of the virtues of the Lord Jesus is the divine attributes. The divine attributes refer to what God is. God is light and love, and God is also patience, holiness, and meekness. All that God is, is His attributes. All these attributes are inherent in God's nature. Then what is God? God is light, love, righteousness, holiness, and patience. When we add all these attributes together, what we have is God. Hence, the law written by God was also written according to His attributes. When the Lord Jesus lived on this earth, He lived a human life, yet what He lived out was not something human but something divine. This means that the divine attributes were lived out of Him to become the virtues of Jesus.

Today, in general, preachers speak only about the virtues of Jesus and do not realize that the virtues of Jesus came out of the intrinsic divine attributes that were in Him. This means that He lived as a man, yet He lived out God. Hence, when He was on the earth, the people around Him, even His followers, such as Peter, James, and John, often asked, "Who is this One?" (Matt. 8:27; 13:53-56; Mark 4:41). They did not know who He was because they did not realize that Christ was God who became a man. Not to mention that today's Christians do not have this realization; even the disciples who followed the Lord Jesus for three and a half years did not have such a realization. They said, "Who is this One? He is clearly a man; He is someone whom we all know; His mother is Mary, and we also know His brothers." Furthermore, according to what is recorded in the Scriptures, the outward form of Jesus was not tall and husky, and His appearance was not comely; rather, He looked poor and lowly (Isa. 53:2; 52:14). These days I have enjoyed singing a very shallow hymn, #1060. The first stanza with the chorus says, "Thou didst leave Thy throne and Thy kingly crown, / When Thou camest to earth for me; / But in Bethlehem's home was there found no room / For Thy holy nativity: / Oh, come to my heart, Lord Jesus! / There is room in my heart for Thee; / Oh, come to my heart, Lord Jesus, come, / There is room in my heart for Thee." My emphasis is on stanza two: "Heaven's arches rang when the angels sang, / Proclaiming Thy royal degree; / But of lowly birth cam'st Thou, Lord, on earth, / And in great humility." What I want to stress is the last two lines: "But of lowly birth cam'st Thou, Lord, on earth, / And in great humility." [Note: In the Chinese version these two lines say: But

You came to earth, born of a poor family, without an attractive form, / Grew up in a humble city, and were esteemed by none—Trans.] I really like these two lines; they are superb. The Lord Jesus was just such a man so that no one would ever think that there was something as a treasure in Him or that God was in Him.

Peter, John, James, Mary, and many others saw the virtues of the Lord Jesus. He endured what others could not. Regardless of how others insulted Him, He was still meek toward them. One time He and His disciples passed through a village, but the people of the entire village did not receive them. So James and John said to the Lord, "Lord, do You want us to command fire to come down from heaven and consume them?" But the Lord Jesus said, "You do not know of what kind of spirit you are" (Luke 9:54-55). That was a virtue. On another occasion, little children were brought to Jesus so that He might lay His hands on them and pray, but the disciples rebuked them. But Jesus said, "Allow the little children and do not prevent them from coming to Me" (Matt. 19:13-14). This also was a virtue. Although they saw the virtues of the Lord Jesus, no one realized that these virtues of His were lived out by Him from all the attributes of divinity in Him. Therefore, in this year's Chinese-speaking conference, the new hymn that I wrote says, "Flesh He became, the first God-man, / His pleasure that I God may be: / In life and nature I'm God's kind, / Though Godhead's His exclusively. / His attributes my virtues are; / His glorious image shines through me." This is the kind of person the Lord Jesus was when He was on the earth. God's attributes became the virtues in Jesus, and God's glorious image was manifested and lived out in Him.

CHRIST AS THE SEED OF DAVID
BECOMING THE SON OF GOD

After the Lord went through His death and resurrection, one of His disciples said to Him, "My Lord and my God!" (John 20:28). Before the resurrection of the Lord Jesus, the disciples addressed Him as Lord. This form of address is about the same as the way the people in the Old Testament addressed God. It was a general title of address among the Jews. However, since the Lord Jesus was a man, how could He be called God? This is because He was incarnated to be a man as the seed of David. This seed of David became the firstborn Son of God in resurrection. This is what Romans 1:1-4 tells us. The truth in Romans 1:1-4 is based on 2 Samuel 7:12-14. David desired to build a house for God, but God said, "Do not build a house for Me; rather, I will make you a house. And out of your house I will raise up a seed for you. I will be his Father, and he will be My son." This corresponds to what Romans 1 says: that the seed of David became the Son of God.

GOD'S FIRSTBORN SON AND GOD'S MANY SONS

When the Bible readers, including the Jewish rabbis, come to 2 Samuel 7:12, they do not try to probe deeply into it. Was He not the seed of David? Then how did He become the Son of God? Concerning this, David gave a clear word in Psalm 2:7. There it says, "You are My Son; / Today I have begotten You." Then in Acts 13:33 Paul gave an explanation of this word saying that it refers to the resurrection of Christ. *Today I have begotten You* means that on the day of resurrection the humanity of Christ was begotten by God to be the Son of God. It was from this day that the Son of God had the human nature within Him. Before that day, before His resurrection, He was merely the only begotten Son of God. As God's only begotten Son, He had only God in Him and the divine essence; He had nothing to do with man. But through His death and in His resurrection, the man whom He had become was brought by God into divinity. This was His being begotten as the first-born Son of God. When humans give birth, it is usually one child per birth. But Christ's birth included a great number, not just one—He Himself. He is the Firstborn, and there are millions and millions of sons after Him. The Bible says clearly that we the saved ones have been resurrected with Him. Hence, 1 Peter 1:3 says, "Blessed be the God and Father of our Lord Jesus Christ, who according to His great mercy has regenerated us unto a living hope through the resurrection of Jesus Christ from the dead." In Christ's resurrection, not only was Christ with His humanity begotten as the firstborn Son, but those who had been chosen by God and redeemed through the death of Christ were born as the many sons of God. Hence, God has the firstborn Son and He also has the many sons. This is clearly told in both the Old Testament and the New Testament. In Romans 8:29 Paul said that God made His Son the Firstborn among many brothers. Hebrews 2:10 says that one day this firstborn Son, as our Captain, will bring us, the many sons, His many brothers, into glory. Hebrews 2:11-12 says that both the firstborn Son and the many sons are all of One and that He is not ashamed to call them brothers, saying, "I will declare Your [the Father's] name to My brothers."

This is the resurrection of Christ. But this resurrection is not simple. In the resurrection of Christ, first, Jesus with His humanity was begotten to be the firstborn Son of God; second, we, the God-chosen and Christ-redeemed people, were begotten to be the many sons of God; and third, the last Adam in His humanity, who is the incarnated Jesus, became the life-giving Spirit. It was the last Adam, the incarnated Jesus, who became the life-giving Spirit; hence, the life-giving Spirit is the very Jesus Christ.

THE CONSUMMATION OF CHRIST'S RESURRECTION BEING THE LIFE-GIVING SPIRIT

Hence, the consummation of Christ's resurrection is that Christ became the life-giving Spirit. The life-giving Spirit is the incarnated Christ, who is the embodiment of the Triune God. Thus, by inference we say that the life-giving Spirit is the all-inclusive Christ, the processed and consummated Triune God. Today this processed Triune God has become the life-giving Spirit. Hence, this life-giving Spirit is the ultimate consummation of the Triune God. From eternity He was the Triune God with all three, the Father, the Son, and the Spirit, but without having gone through the processes. What are the processes that He went through? They are the processes of incarnation, human living, crucifixion, and resurrection. In eternity the Triune God had no human element, no experiences of human living, no element of death, and no element of resurrection. Hence, He could not be considered completed. He was eternally complete but was not completed. However, the Spirit is the ultimate consummation of the Triune God. At this point the Triune God is fully completed. He is the God-man having humanity and the human living, and He passed through death and entered into resurrection. Now He has these four great elements—humanity, the experience of human living, death, and resurrection—which were not in the Triune God in eternity.

MAN BECOMING GOD,
HAVING GOD'S LIFE AND NATURE

Who is Christ? Christ is not only the Creator but also a created one. The early theologians all believed this, but the latter theologians did not dare to teach this. "God becoming man and man becoming God" was very prevailing in ancient times. Hence, early in the fourth century Athanasius, who was present at the Nicene Council, said that "He was made man that we might be made God." Actually, this word means that God became a man in order to make all of us, His believers, God. This had already been spoken in the second century, but, later, people did not have the boldness to say this. What God created was a man, but that man had the image of God. Eventually, God would come in to beget men to be His children, having His life and nature. Hence, man is of God's kind in life and nature.

What is wrong with saying that man becomes God? However, I am very careful in saying this. Those in the early days taught this not as clearly and carefully as we do today. I especially point out that man becomes God without sharing the Godhead but having only God's life and nature. Not one teacher in Christianity can oppose this. Once we believe in the Lord, we receive God's life, and 2 Peter 1:4 says clearly that we can "become partakers of the divine nature." No one can refute this. First John 3:2 tells us, "We know that if He is manifested, we will be like Him because we will see Him even as He is." I hope that we can definitely lay a good groundwork for this among us.

THE STEPS GOD TOOK TO MAKE MAN GOD

God became man through the process of being incarnated, living a human life, being crucified, and entering into resurrection. How does God make man God? First, God became a man. The process which God went through from incarnation to resurrection was the procedure for Him to become man. Eventually in His resurrection He became the life-giving Spirit. In this Spirit He comes to carry out the work of making man God. First, He is now the sanctifying Spirit, as we are told in 1 Peter 1:2. We were people fallen into sin, but some believers were moved by God to come and preach the gospel to us. Through the preaching of the gospel this sanctifying Spirit comes to separate us, the God-chosen people. The Spirit's sanctifying work on the sinners is like the woman's lighting a lamp and seeking carefully for the lost coin, as recorded in Luke 15 (v. 8). We were sanctified before we were saved. Second, at the time we heard the gospel, the Spirit put faith into us. Third, when we believed, the life of God, which is God Himself, Christ Himself, entered into us. Thus we were regenerated.

The sanctification we experience after our regeneration is not positional sanctification but dispositional sanctification. When the Spirit separated us from sinners, that was the positional sanctification that took place before we were saved. When the Spirit comes into us to change our disposition, that is the dispositional sanctification that takes place after our regeneration. This dispositional sanctification is not accomplished in one day. This sanctification issues in renewing, which is a lifelong matter. Renewing issues in transformation, which is also a lifelong matter. The final result of transformation is to be conformed to the image of the Lord and be the same as He is. From the first step of regeneration to the final step of conformation, everything is carried out by the Spirit. Eventually, this Spirit will bring us into glory so that God will be completely expressed from within us through our corrupted body. At that time, our corrupted body will also be redeemed and transformed. That is glorification, as spoken of in Romans 8:30: "Those whom He justified, these He also glorified." It is by these steps that God is making us God.

THE REALITY OF THE BODY OF CHRIST

Now we go on to see the reality of the Body of Christ. The reality of the Body of Christ is the Spirit, and the Spirit is the resurrection. Brother Nee made a statement, saying that "the Holy Spirit is the reality of resurrection; without the Holy Spirit, there is no resurrection." In John 11:25 the Lord Jesus said, "I am the resurrection and the life." He is not only the life but also the resurrection. However, most of us can understand that the Spirit is life, but we cannot comprehend that the Spirit is resurrection. The Lord Jesus said that He is the resurrection. What is this resurrection? This resurrection is the ultimate consummation of the Triune God. The work of the Triune God in us is to produce the Body of Christ, the reality of which is the Spirit, the pneumatic Christ. This Spirit as the consummated Triune God, the resurrection, works in us. When we have the pneumatic Christ, the consummated Triune God, the resurrection, we are practically the Body of Christ. Without this, neither the local church nor the elders and the deacons are the Body of Christ. The local church and the elders and deacons are used by the Lord to lead the children of God who are still living in the flesh, the physical body.

We are still in the flesh, and in the flesh we need to live and we need a place to live in. Furthermore, whenever we come together we should not act improperly; rather, we should behave in an orderly manner. Therefore, we need the elders and the deacons. But these are not the diamond itself; they are merely the wrapping for the diamond. Moreover, the diamond needs a box to hold it. Therefore, in the local churches all the elders and deacons and all the practices are just the outward wrapping and the box; they cannot be brought to the New Jerusalem. We do not need to argue about things such as the autonomy of the local church and the local boundary. Although the local churches are independent of each other in business affairs, they all are one in the matter of the treasure. What is the treasure? It is the testimony of

Jesus. Today how can we produce this treasure? It is by Christ having accomplished everything and ascended to the heavens. Today, in His ascension, as the Minister in heaven He is working into us, bit by bit, everything that He has accomplished, from His incarnation to His resurrection.

Today we do not need to continue to preach the old teachings as the outward wrappings. We do not need to argue about the superficial things. As long as the treasure is here, it is good enough. When you package the treasure, whether you package it this way or that way is not worth arguing about. Whether you package it this way or that way, it is still the same gem. Whether you put two layers or three layers of wrapping around it, it is the same gem. Even if you do not put any wrapping around it, it is still the same gem. As long as this gem is here, it is good enough. As long as we can experience Christ, it is all right; there is nothing to argue about. Whether immersion, sprinkling, hot water, cold water, sea water, or fresh water, nothing matters. Therefore, we need to have a thorough seeing. All that is worthwhile is the Spirit. We should allow the Spirit to come into us and let the cross of Christ be practically put into us. This is what is worthwhile. This is the treasure.

Where are we today? Today we are not throwing away all the outward things; we still keep the outward things. But we keep the outward things not according to what we like. We keep them according to the examples shown in the Bible. The example given in the Bible for baptism is by immersion. So, we baptize people into water. We do not necessarily baptize people in a baptistery. We just put people into water; even in a bathtub is all right. We should not be legal. The outward things are not worth our attention. We need to pay attention to the treasure within. When we see the treasure within, we will not be divided. As long as we are divided, we no longer see the treasure. Hence, the reality of the Body of Christ is the consummated Triune God within us, who is the pneumatic Christ, the resurrection. May the Lord have mercy on us to turn us from the outward things to the reality.

CHAPTER FOUR

THE REALITY OF THE BODY OF CHRIST

(2)

Prayer: Lord, our heart is full of thanks for Your recovery. In this age You have revealed to us Your recovery, and You have also entrusted us with Your recovery, charging us to spread Your recovery throughout the whole world. Lord, because of Your mercy and Your grace, You have truly carried it out to this extent. Lord, we sense, however, that up to this day we are still very short and we are weak in many ways. We have not lived like God-men sufficiently in our life, walk, and work on this earth. O Lord, we pray that You will open our eyes again tonight that within us we may see clearly that the reality of the Body of Christ is the living of God and man together. Oh, we really look to You for Your blessing and for Your speaking a clear word to us. We also pray that You will deliver us from superfluous words and give us the pure words, the purified words. Amen.

Concerning the reality of the Body of Christ, I sense that the burden within me is still not discharged. So, tonight we still need to speak about this matter. Afterward, we will speak a word of warning and caution.

THE REALITY OF THE BODY OF CHRIST—
THE LIVING TOGETHER OF GOD AND MAN

Simply, the reality of the Body of Christ is the living of a God-man life by a group of God-redeemed people together with the God-man Christ. Before the incarnation, crucifixion, and resurrection of Christ, in the universe there was God in heaven and man on the earth. But in the universe there was not one human being who was both God and man. Furthermore, this One who was to be God yet man did not become a man in the twinkling of an eye. Rather, according to man's natural law, He was conceived in His mother's womb for nine months, and then He was born to be a man. He lived on this earth for thirty-three and a half years, beginning as a child. In the past I had a question concerning this matter: Why did the Lord have to live on the earth for such a long time? He lived on the earth for thirty-three and a half years, and it seems that it was in the last three and a half years, when He came out to do the preaching and to lead the disciples, that He was really doing the work of God. Concerning the first thirty years of the Lord's life on earth, the Gospels do not say much. However, we can find out that He lived in a poor carpenter's home and He was called a carpenter (Matt. 13:55; Mark 6:3). I did not understand, however, what the significance was of the Lord's living the life of a carpenter for thirty years on the earth. Now, because of the shining of the light, I have seen that He used those thirty-three and a half years to live out the model of a God-man living.

After His death and resurrection He produced many brothers who, with Him as the oldest Brother, become the one great man in the universe. What is this great, universal man? This is a God-man, one who is God yet man and man yet God. First, He lived on the earth to live out a model. How did He as the God-man live? He had the life of man, and He definitely was a man on the earth. He hungered, He thirsted, He slept, and He even wept and shed tears and was tired and weary. Not only was He like a man, but He was a man. However, as a man, He lived not by the human life but by the divine life within Him. He lived, yet He did not live alone. He lived not by His own life but by the divine life. He told us clearly that He spoke and did things not by Himself but by the One who sent Him (John 5:19; 8:28). In John 6:57 He said, "The living Father has sent Me and I live because of the Father." But for what purpose did the living Father send Him? In general, Christians would spontaneously reply that the Father sent Him to be our Savior and to accomplish redemption for us. Perhaps they would go on to say that He came to bring God's life to us. There is nothing wrong in saying this, but it is altogether a superficial statement. What was the purpose of

God in sending the Lord Jesus? God sent Him to be a man and to live a God-man life by the divine life. This kind of living issues in a universal great man that is exactly the same as He is—a man living a God-man life by the divine life. I earnestly hope that you will clearly remember the Lord's word in John 6:57. For what purpose did God send the Lord Jesus? If you read the entire Gospel of John, you will know the meaning of this verse. God sent Him to be a man and to live a God-man life by the divine life. He lived on the earth for thirty-three and a half years and produced a model of such a living. At the end of this life He went to die on the cross, and then He passed through death and resurrection. In His resurrection He brought His human nature into God and was begotten by God as the firstborn Son of God. Not only so, in His resurrection all the God-chosen ones were born together with Him in His birth. Ephesians 2:5-6 tells us that God "made us alive together with Christ…and raised us up together with Him.…" This making alive and raising up is the begetting. How do we know? Because in Acts 13:33 we are told that when God raised Jesus from the dead, He said to Him, "You are My Son; today I have begotten You." On what day did the begetting take place? It took place on the day of the Lord's resurrection. Hence, when the resurrection was accomplished, the firstborn Son of God and the many sons of God all were begotten. As such a One He became a life-giving Spirit (1 Cor. 15:45b) and brought forth Himself and the many sons of God in resurrection.

The Lord Jesus resurrected and ascended to the heavens, and He is now in heaven as the life-giving Spirit. This life-giving Spirit is the One who is God yet man, who was incarnated, passed through human living, died, and was resurrected. After regenerating us, the life-giving Spirit dwells in us and is mingled with our spirit to live a God-man life with us. He is the very One who is God yet man and who died and was resurrected to become the life-giving Spirit, the pneumatic Christ. In His ascension He is the Mediator of the new covenant (Heb. 8:6), the surety of the new covenant (7:22), the High Priest (8:1), and the heavenly Minister (v. 2).

Now in the heavens He is doing one thing, that is, to work on all His redeemed and regenerated people to make them God. How does He do it? He does it by being in them to continuously sanctify them, renew them, and transform them. This transformation is to deify them.

The purpose of transformation is to make man God until man is conformed to the image of God and is exactly like God (2 Cor. 3:18). The image of God is the One who is God yet man. It is true that He lived on earth as a man, but He did not live by His human life; rather, He lived by God as His life. Therefore, He rejected and denied Himself. During His thirty-three and a half years on earth, every day He lived a life by God, a life in which He rejected and denied Himself. This kind of life is a life lived under the cross by the resurrection life. Therefore, as far as Christ is concerned, before He went to the cross to die and be resurrected, every day He lived a life of death and resurrection. To die is to reject ourselves and put ourselves to death; to be resurrected is to live out God as our life. Although what is lived out is a human life, the virtues that are manifested are something transformed from the divine attributes.

THE LIVING OF JESUS ON THE EARTH BEING A MODEL OF A LIVING SHARED BY GOD AND MAN

When the Lord Jesus lived on the earth, He was genuinely a man, but instead of living by the life of man He lived by God as His life. Thus, in His life and in His living He lived the divine attributes as His human virtues manifested before the eyes of men. When people looked at Him, outwardly they saw that He was really a man. However, the more they observed Him and the more they followed Him, the more they had to admit that He truly was God. In the four Gospels we see the Galileans who followed the Lord for three and a half years. In the beginning they realized that He was the son of a carpenter, that He was a man. Gradually, the more they observed Him, the more they saw the virtues that were manifested in the Lord Jesus. Those virtues could never have been something of man. Where did those virtues come from? In those days the Galileans did not know, but today we know that those virtues were lived out of the God-man Jesus, who as a man lived not by Himself but by God and who lived out the divine attributes and manifested them as the virtues of such a One who is God yet man.

After the Lord Jesus was resurrected from the dead, His disciples also understood. At that time they began to realize that Christ is God. They had this realization not only because they saw the miracles He did, such as His calming the winds and the sea and raising the dead. Rather, they realized that He is God because they saw the attributes of the very nature of God lived out through a man to become the very virtues of that man. No doubt, God is in the virtues of Christ as a man. Therefore, at the end of the Gospels we can see that, unlike today's Christians in their general situation, the disciples had a very deep and high realization of Him as God.

In His death and resurrection Christ also produced us. He brought God into us not in an objective way but in a subjective way. As He had brought God into Mary, so also now He brought God into us, His redeemed ones. In this way He began to make us God; that is, He begot us as children of God. Since we were born of God the Father in Christ, and since our Father God is God, how can we, the children begotten of Him, not be God? Since our Father is God, we who are born of Him surely also are God.

However, although we have been born in this way, we are still the old creation and we are still in our flesh. We are still natural and we still have our old "I." At the same time, we must also admit that we are still filthy and corrupt. We live in the world and are constantly contaminated by the filthiness of this world. What then shall we do? Generally, Christians are taught that Jesus is the almighty Lord and the One who is the same yesterday, today, and forever, and that He is in heaven today praying for us and is able to save us to the uttermost. But what God shows us is that although such teachings are good, they are superficial and not quite accurate. Christians know that Christ intercedes in heaven for us and sympathizes with us in our problems by rendering help to us in the environment. However, in reality, it is not like that. Actually, this ascended God-man is both God and man.

He is man, not the man who was created and became fallen, but the man who was created and who went through death and resurrection and was uplifted. He is such a man now in resurrection. At the same time, He is also God, but He is not the God who is purely God, the God before His incarnation. Now this God is the consummated God. Within Him are God, man, human experience, the effectiveness of death, and the power of resurrection. All these elements are compounded together to become one compounded Spirit. There is a clear type of this in the Old Testament in Exodus 30:23-29. A hin of olive oil was compounded with four kinds of spices—myrrh, cinnamon, calamus, and cassia—making a total of five ingredients. This signifies that the Spirit of God is compounded with Christ's death and its effectiveness and also with Christ's resurrection and its power. All these elements are compounded together to become a compound anointing ointment. It is not just oil but an ointment. The tabernacle, the serving priests of God, and everything related to the worship of God were anointed with this anointing ointment.

THE LIVING OF MAN BECOMING GOD BEING A LIVING OF DEATH AND RESURRECTION UNDER THE CROSS

After the Lord practically lived out a typical God-man, He accomplished redemption through His death and resurrection to redeem us and regenerate us to be the same as He is. We are of the same life and nature as He. In this way we become God and we become the children of God. However, we still have many negative things in us. Thank the Lord, He dealt with all these negative things in His death. He went to the cross with our flesh and with our sinful human nature. We all were dealt with by Him on the cross. Our old man has been crucified with Him; thus, the old creation, the flesh, Satan, and the world, that is, everything involved with the old man, were also dealt with on the cross. Today, since we have been regenerated, we should no longer participate in or live by these things. Rather, we should reject our self as the Lord Jesus denied His self. Our self is corrupt, even corrupt to the extent of being incurable. Christ has not one bit of evil in Him and He is absolutely good, yet He had to put

aside His good self. This being the case, how much more do we
need to put aside our evil self. Therefore, today, if we desire to
have the reality of the Body of Christ, we must live the
God-man life. To live the God-man life, we need to receive the
cross.

Stanza one of hymn #631 in *Hymns* says, "If I'd know
Christ's risen power, / I must ever love the Cross; / Life from
death alone arises; / There's no gain except by loss." Stanza
two says, "If I'd have Christ formed within me, / I must
breathe my final breath, / Live within the Cross's shadow, /
Put my soul-life e'er to death." If we know the power of resurrection, we will surely be delighted to be in the mold of the
cross and to be conformed to it. Hence, Philippians 3:10 says
that it is through the resurrection power of Christ that we are
conformed to the death of Christ. By ourselves we cannot be
conformed to Christ's death; by ourselves we cannot deny ourselves. We are conformed to the death of Christ by the power
of His resurrection, which is not a thing or a matter but a
person, the life-giving Spirit.

The life-giving Spirit is the compound Spirit, the pneumatic
Christ, the consummation of the processed and consummated
Triune God. This is resurrection. The Lord clearly said that
He is the resurrection (John 11:25). Therefore, resurrection
is the consummation of the Triune God, the pneumatic
Christ, who accomplished redemption for us and who is the
life-giving Spirit indwelling us. Today He lives in us to
dispense the divine life into us daily. This divine life is the
life of the One who is God yet man, the life that was lived out
by the One who was God incarnated to be a man and who
became the God-man, not by His human life but by His divine
life.

NO LONGER I LIVING ALONE,
BUT GOD LIVING TOGETHER WITH ME

The way for us to live out a God-man is by death and
resurrection. We are dying every moment of every day, and
we are living every moment of every day by the indwelling
life-giving Spirit. According to my experience as a Christian,
in the beginning, before I had received any help from Brother

Nee, although I was pursuing, I did not know anything regarding what the experience of life is. I was taught by the Brethren for seven and a half years, but all those teachings were outward, superficial things. From the time I came into contact with Brother Nee, I knew I needed to die, I needed to remain on the cross, and I needed to live according to the Spirit. Gradually, in the Lord's recovery the Lord has shown me that this is not all and that this is not sufficient. We still need to see that the Christian life which the Lord desires is one in which we are all day long, every minute and every second, under death, having one life and one living with the indwelling Triune God, the pneumatic Christ, the life-giving Spirit. This is why stanza three of the new hymn says, "No longer I alone that live, / But God together lives with me."

Concerning this matter, there is a wrong teaching in Christianity. Some say that we Christians live an exchanged life. They say that our life is very bad, so Christ nailed it on the cross, and in exchange, Christ Himself comes to live in us; hence, it is a matter of an exchange in life. This kind of teaching is wrong. We were crucified on the cross, but that crucifixion was not our end; rather, we were resurrected. It is true that Galatians 2:20 does say that we are crucified with Christ, yet we did not stop there but were resurrected with Christ. On the one hand, I was terminated; on the other hand, the resurrected "I" still lives. I did not hand myself over in exchange for another life. Rather, the old "I" was uplifted, and Christ is living in the new "I." This is why, on the one hand, Paul said that he was crucified with Christ and was terminated, but on the other hand, he went on also to say that "I...live." "It is no longer I who live," but this does not mean that there is no more I, because "I now live." How do I live? I live by exercising the faith of the Son of God; that is, I live by Christ Himself. "No longer I" does not mean that I am no more; it means that I who live by myself am no more. When we say that we are crucified with Christ, it does not mean that Christ comes in to replace us and there is no more I. This kind of interpretation is wrong.

CHRIST LIVING, AND
WE ALSO LIVING BECAUSE OF HIM

In John 14:16-17 the Lord Jesus said to His disciples, "I will ask the Father, and He will give you another Comforter, that He may be with you forever, even the Spirit of reality...." Then in verse 19 He said, "...because I live, you also shall live." It was on the day of resurrection that the disciples knew that the Lord lived and they also lived. But the way they lived was different from the way they had lived before they had been crucified with Christ. Whereas formerly they had lived by their own life, now after they had been crucified with Christ, they lived by the life of the Triune God, who had resurrected them. In John 6:57 even Christ, who was sent by God, said, "As the living Father has sent Me and I live because of the Father...." Christ lived because of the Father. This means that Christ did not live by Himself. It is difficult to determine the meaning of the word *because* in Greek. Some versions translated the word "by." However, this is a wrong translation. In his translation Darby has a note on this word saying that the word here is not simply "by" or "through" or "on account of." The Lord was sent by the Father with a commission, that is, to live out the Father. Hence, since the Lord was sent by the Father, He came to live out the Father. It was for this reason that the Father sent the Son. Furthermore, Darby said that here it refers to what the Father is and His living. The Father has what He is and His living. The Son was sent with the commission to live out what the Father is and His living. In John 6:57 the Lord went on to say, "So he who eats Me, he also shall live because of Me." To live because of the Lord is to live out what the Lord is and His living.

Christ was resurrected, and the Spirit came into us. Since that time, because He lives, we also live. He lives, and we also live because of Him. This is because He and we, we and He, live together. Therefore, in resurrection He and we, we and He, are altogether joined and mingled as one. Hence, Paul said, "To me, to live is Christ" (Phil. 1:21). Moreover, he said, "...as always, even now Christ will be magnified in my body" (v. 20). It was Paul who lived, but it was Christ, not Paul, who was manifested. When Jesus lived, what was manifested was not Jesus nor a carpenter from Nazareth, but God. In the human virtues of Jesus the divine attributes were manifested. What was lived out was the God-man as the issue of the union and mingling of God with man. This God-man was enlarged in the resurrection of Christ. Whereas formerly this God-man consisted of one Son, now he has been enlarged to be the firstborn Son and many sons. This enlargement is an organism, which is the Body of Christ.

THE REALITY OF THE BODY OF CHRIST
BEING THE UNION AND MINGLING OF GOD WITH MAN
TO LIVE OUT A CORPORATE GOD-MAN

The Body of Christ is not merely a term but a reality. The reality of the Body of Christ is the union and mingling of God with man to live out a corporate God-man. For this we need to pass through death and resurrection, dying daily and being resurrected daily. We also need to be in the Spirit and walk according to the Spirit daily.

Again, let me speak something of my own experience. For many years I have felt that I am quite all right, but recently the Lord showed me differently. I have been telling the brothers and sisters that the people of God are God's wife and that they should take God as their Husband, and I have presented this in a very clear and reasonable way. Yet, in reality, instead of taking God as the Husband, I have been taking myself as the husband in my living. It is according to moral standards that I do not do bad things or speak bad words to my wife. Yet, I do not take God as my Husband and speak by Him. I myself am the husband, and I speak by myself and speak concerning the work by myself. Recently, because of the great vision that I saw, I have been practicing one thing, that is, when I am going to speak to others, within me I ask, "Is it you who wants to speak, or is it your Husband?" In other words, "Is it you who wants to speak, or is it the Spirit who dwells in you? Is your speaking in the Spirit and according to the Spirit?" If we use this standard to weigh or measure ourselves, we will see that we are far below the standard. Although we have seen the vision concerning the Body of Christ and can speak clearly about it, what we have as the reality of the Body of Christ is very little.

THE ONENESS OF THE BODY BEING THE SPIRIT

What we do and speak in the meetings mostly is not the reality of the Body of Christ. What we have mostly is merely some outward matters. We have the local churches, and we know how to set up churches, how to appoint elders, and how to assign deacons. We also know how to have good meetings by not having one man speaking but having everyone practicing to prophesy as prophets. All these things are correct and right, but are they carried out in the Spirit and according to the Spirit? My answer is that for the most part they are not. Hence, even in the Lord's recovery we are very lacking in the reality of the Body of Christ.

The way to live out the reality of the Body of Christ is to go through death and resurrection by the living together of God with man. Through death everything on our side was cleared up; through resurrection our human nature was uplifted and we were begotten to be the many sons of God. Although we are God's children today, we still have a great number of negative things hanging on us. Hence, every day we must stay with the cross. We must die every day and every moment; everything must die.

Whether you are going to tell people that the local churches are not autonomous, or you are going to tell people that, on the one hand, the local churches are autonomous and, on the other hand, they are joined as one Body, you must speak in the reality of the Body of Christ, that is, in the Spirit. To be sure, it is not accurate to say that the local churches are absolutely autonomous; to be sure, it is correct to say that, on the one hand, the local churches are autonomous and, on the other hand, they are joined as the universal Body of Christ. Nevertheless, in principle, those who speak these things speak in themselves; they do not speak in the Spirit or according to the Spirit. Hence, what they speak is meaningless. If you see this light, you do not have to say anything, and yet you will spontaneously keep the oneness of the Body. How do we keep the oneness of the Body? What is this oneness?

This oneness is the Spirit. Hence, Ephesians 4:4 says, "One Body and one Spirit." This is the oneness of the Body. When you are in the Spirit, you keep this oneness; when you are not in the Spirit, even if you say you are not divided, you are divided.

A WORD OF WARNING AND CAUTION

Now I would like to speak a word of warning and caution. We need to be on the alert because we all have ambition; there is no one who is without ambition. That which is most harmful to us, most obstructive to God, most damaging to the Lord's recovery, and most destructive to the Body of Christ is our ambition. On the one hand, everyone desires to be an elder or to be an apostle or, at the very least, to be a deacon, and if not a deacon, to be one who takes the lead. On the other hand, in our working for the Lord we aspire to have the top preaching, to preach better than others; we also aspire to have a more powerful work than others, to bring more people to salvation than others, to have the church under our leadership excel over other churches. All the seeds of division are found in ambition. When ambition is gone, all divisions are gone.

In my working together with Brother Nee, the first thing I noticed in him is that he was a person without ambition. He knew only to work; he had no ambition. Hence, I was very much influenced by him. In my sixty years in the Lord's recovery I have had no ambition. You can trace my history: whether in Chefoo, in Shanghai, or in Taiwan, I had no ambition. I knew only to toil and labor. After I finished the work, when the Lord led me to leave, I just left.

Let us look back on the history of the Lord's recovery among us. All those who were ambitious and therefore dissenting, rebellious, and divisive, whether in mainland China or in Taiwan—where are they today? In those days the dissenting ones in Taiwan said that they had seen the vision and that the leading co-workers had become old and were ready to be put in a coffin. But today I would like to ask, What happened to their vision? I warned them, saying, "Once you leave this ground, you will divide again and again; you will divide endlessly." My word has been fulfilled. Among the four or five of them, no two are together; some have returned to the world to get a job, and the whereabouts of the others are unknown. While I am writing the outlines of 1 and 2 Kings, I see God's judgment on everyone, and His judgment is severe. As to the four leading rebellious ones in recent times, what are they doing today? They have no message to give and no work to do. All they do is go to different places to attack me and spread rumors, creating divisions everywhere.

I would like us to see these histories and learn lessons from the failures of those who preceded us. Beginning with Brother Nee, everyone who has been faithful and sincere to stay in the Lord's recovery has been blessed. Even if they have not had much gift, they have brought in the Lord's blessing. These are things that I want to bring out as a warning.

Now concerning being cautious, we must never allow our self, our natural being, our old "I," and our disposition to be resurrected. In the Lord's work we do not have ambition, comparison, competition, or envy. Furthermore, we will never look at others' mistakes, but always consider others more excellent than ourselves. Do not boast in what you have accomplished nor be envious of what others have done nor judge others' errors. Even if you are fully aware that what others do is wrong and that there are shortcomings, not only should you not criticize them but you should even help them. We are not sent by the Lord to measure others with a measuring stick. Rather, we are sent by Him to minister Christ to people. We must learn to be humble. If there is something that others have and we do not have, we should receive it with a humble heart. Everyone has shortcomings, but we are not sent by the Lord to expose others' shortcomings. We are sent by Him to minister life and to minister Christ to others.

Finally, in doing the Lord's work we only labor. We should not attempt to show off and boast concerning our work. We should not be reluctant to give up our work, nor take credit for our success. When we leave, we simply leave and turn over everything to others. We conduct ourselves in this way—without ambition, without self-boasting, without making comparisons, and without blaming others for their mistakes—because we have seen the Body. Consequently, what we are doing today is not our personal work but the economy of God throughout the generations, that is, the building up of the Body of Christ. The Lord can cause us to live out the life of a God-man by our being joined with others. Hence, the third stanza of our new hymn says, "No longer I alone that live, / But God together lives with me. / Built with the saints in the Triune God, / His universal house we'll be, / And His organic Body we / For His expression corp'rately." This is the reality of the Body of Christ.

If we have seen this, we will not pay attention to the outward practices. Whatever you do is of the old creation unless it goes through death and resurrection. If you do it right, it is of the old creation; if you do it wrong, it is also of the old creation. Both are of no value. In our service to God, first, we must see that God is not mocked. Second, we must see that in the universe God has not only the laws on the physical side but also the laws on the spiritual side; moreover, the spiritual laws are stricter than the physical laws. Hence, once we touch the spiritual work of God, we must be restricted by His laws. If we deviate just a little from His laws, we are finished. This is like running on a racecourse. When you run, you must stay within two lines; once you step on the white line, you are out-of-bounds; and even if you regret it, there is no remedy. This is true. In the past I said these things to the dissenting ones, warning them that they should by no means create any division or be rebellious. To this day, I have rarely seen a rebellious one repent.

Whatever you do, whether you preach the gospel or go to the villages or come to the United States or carry out a training, never consider that you are doing something more excellent than others. Furthermore, do not compare yourself with others so that you are discouraged because you sense that you are not doing as well as others. We should have none of these things. We only know that we should labor, that we should die daily and be resurrected daily, and that we should daily walk in the Spirit, that is, according to the Spirit. As to the rest, I can testify here that it is the Lord's responsibility.

ABOUT THE AUTHOR

Witness Lee was born in 1905 in northern China and raised in a Christian family. At age 19 he was fully captured for Christ and immediately consecrated himself to preach the gospel for the rest of his life. Early in his service, he met Watchman Nee, a renowned preacher, teacher, and writer. Witness Lee labored together with Watchman Nee under his direction. In 1934 Watchman Nee entrusted Witness Lee with the responsibility for his publication operation, called the Shanghai Gospel Bookroom.

Prior to the Communist takeover in 1949, Witness Lee was sent by Watchman Nee and his other co-workers to Taiwan to ensure that the things delivered to them by the Lord would not be lost. Watchman Nee instructed Witness Lee to continue the former's publishing operation abroad as the Taiwan Gospel Bookroom, which has been publicly recognized as the publisher of Watchman Nee's works outside China. Witness Lee's work in Taiwan manifested the Lord's abundant blessing. From a mere 350 believers, newly fled from the mainland, the churches in Taiwan grew to 20,000 in five years.

In 1962 Witness Lee felt led of the Lord to come to the United States, settling in California. During his 35 years of service in the U.S., he ministered in weekly meetings and weekend conferences, delivering several thousand spoken messages. Much of his speaking has since been published as over 400 titles. Many of these have been translated into over fourteen languages. He gave his last public conference in February 1997 at the age of 91.

He leaves behind a prolific presentation of the truth in the Bible. His major work, *Life-study of the Bible,* comprises over 25,000 pages of commentary on every book of the Bible from the perspective of the believers' enjoyment and experience of God's divine life in Christ through the Holy Spirit. Witness Lee was the chief editor of a new translation of the New Testament into Chinese called the Recovery Version and directed the translation of the same into English. The Recovery Version also appears in a number of other languages. He provided an extensive body of footnotes, outlines, and spiritual cross references. A radio broadcast of his messages can be heard on Christian radio stations in the United States. In 1965 Witness Lee founded Living Stream Ministry, a non-profit corporation, located in Anaheim, California, which officially presents his and Watchman Nee's ministry.

Witness Lee's ministry emphasizes the experience of Christ as life and the practical oneness of the believers as the Body of Christ. Stressing the importance of attending to both these matters, he led the churches under his care to grow in Christian life and function. He was unbending in his conviction that God's goal is not narrow sectarianism but the Body of Christ. In time, believers began to meet simply as the church in their localities in response to this conviction. In recent years a number of new churches have been raised up in Russia and in many eastern European countries.